7/15

Sk

CW00797059

Suffolk Libraries

Please return/renew this item
by the last date shown.

**Suffolk Libraries
01473 263838
www.suffolklibraries.co.uk**

30127 08337168 7

Robert Hume

Thomas Crapper

Lavatory Legend

Illustrated by
Cheryl Ives

First published in 2009

Stone Publishing House
17 Stone House
North Foreland Road
Broadstairs
Kent CT10 3NT

www.stonepublishinghouse.com

ISBN: 978-0-9549909-3-0

Typeset in 12pt Garamond by Troubador Publishing Ltd, Leicester, UK
Printed in Great Britain by TJ International, Padstow, Cornwall

For my students –
past, present and future

Chapter 1

South London, 8th February 1887. As Thomas waited at home in a state of nerves, he thought he heard a carriage. From somewhere outside, a loose object flapped against the wall. He checked the time on his pocket watch. Surely it must be half past eight by now, the time he had been told the carriage would arrive to take him to the most important interview of his life. His business, even the future of his family, would depend on what happened today. For he had been summoned to Buckingham Palace by Queen Victoria's eldest son, the Prince of Wales – the man who would one day be King of Great Britain.

Normally, Thomas's working day would begin with a short walk from his home to Clapham Junction railway station. From there he would catch a train to Victoria station, and then board the omnibus to his factory in Chelsea. But today was no ordinary day as we are about to see.

Finally, at eight-thirty, an imposing carriage drew up outside his front door in Middleton Road and a silver-haired man in red livery jumped down from the back. Thomas checked his appearance one final time in the hall mirror. He was pleased with what he saw: his white shirt was spotless (his wife, Maria, had seen to that), the ends of his thin bow-tie were tucked under his stiff collar, his beard which he had grown when he was a young man, was neatly trimmed. (He told his friends that he did not really like his beard but that it kept throat infections away!) When he looked down he saw well-pressed trousers and highly-polished black shoes. As Maria adjusted his hat, her hands trembled: she was just as nervous as her husband.

'Goodbye my dear.' She kissed him. 'I shall be thinking of you!'

Cane in hand, as always, he descended the short flight of steps to the street, turning up his coat collar against the chill air. The coachman pulled open the door and bowed as Thomas climbed the steps into the carriage.

As they left Clapham Common behind and headed north, he seemed to be more aware than usual of all those little details that usually passed him by unnoticed on his walk to catch the train – a little girl selling boxes of matches on Battersea Rise; a row of boys on Lavender Hill cleaning gentlemen's shoes; an old man playing a mouth organ outside Clapham Junction station.

The Albert Bridge was closed for repairs so they crossed the Thames by the Victoria Bridge. The road was narrow and the carriage wheels juddered on the uneven surface. Below them, the water was pale brown and partly obscured by a misty vapour. Soon, Lower Sloane Street joined into the King's Road, and they were forced to slow down because of all the carts and barrows obstructing the way. As they continued eastwards along Hobart Place and Bressenden Place and drew close to Buckingham Palace, they could see that no flag was flying from the roof, which meant the Queen was not in residence. She was probably at Windsor Castle where she spent most of her time since her husband's death almost thirty years ago. But Thomas was not going to see the Queen. His appointment was with her son, the Prince of Wales, who had earned something of a reputation as a playboy, due to his mistresses, drinking and gambling.

The carriage rattled into the grounds of Buckingham Palace and swerved sharply round to the right towards the tradesmen's entrance. Thomas could see the door opening and a footman walking towards the carriage door. He was dressed, like the coachman, in red livery with gleaming gold buttons and white gloves. The footman made a little bow and escorted Thomas into a large reception hall where he was told to wait.

After a while the footman reappeared and led him through a door and up a wide staircase. At the top they crossed a landing and proceeded down a long corridor. Servants with starched aprons and white caps emerged from rooms on either side of the corridor, carrying piles of linen; others walked by briskly, ignoring him, looking straight ahead.

At last they reached a room with huge windows framed with blue velvet curtains. There was silverware and antique vases on display in glass cabinets, and portraits of members of the royal family on the wall. A shaft of bright sunlight glanced across the floor and made the gold picture frames sparkle.

Thomas was motioned to one of the three chairs by the doorway. On the far side of the room a pair of footmen stood like statues guarding a door. As he sat, the slightest sound sent his pulse racing – the click of a key being turned in a lock; and through the open window he could hear a wheelbarrow being drawn along the gravel in the gardens below. There were also long periods of complete silence.

Thomas had started the day with a spring in his

step, brimming with confidence. But that confidence was now beginning to ebb away and the waiting was becoming torture to him. So much was at stake. The contract, should he get it, was so huge that it made his eyes pop out even to think of it! He hoped that he would be able to speak when he was spoken to, and that he would give a good account of himself.

Eventually, the door opened at the far end of the room and a valet beckoned him across. Thomas was tempted to cross the room in great strides but he resisted; he knew it would not be proper. As he drew close the valet spoke:

'His Royal Highness would be much obliged if you would now present yourself, Mr Crapper!'

Thomas was escorted into a room with a high ceiling and walls covered in dark red wallpaper with a gold pattern; all around him there was highly polished furniture. He tried not to stare – he knew it was bad manners – but he could not stop himself. Facing him, standing with his back to a roaring log fire, was a man of similar age to himself, possibly a little younger, maybe in his late forties, with a beard just like his own. A huge pot belly poked through his suit coat, the bottom button of which appeared to be under considerable strain.

Thomas bowed.

As he raised his head, he saw bloodshot eyes and blotchy skin. Thomas thought of the Prince of Wales's wild reputation. Was he suffering from a hangover? And there were other clues in the room to back up this impression, above all a lingering smell of brandy and stale cigar smoke, which some recent polishing had failed to conceal.

'Your Royal Highness,' Thomas began.

Then he remembered: he should have waited for the Prince to speak first.

An awkward silence followed.

The Prince of Wales stared at him with intense, protruding eyes.

'Mr Crapper, please take a seat, over there by the window.'

Thomas went across and sat down. The Prince of Wales remained standing.

'Mr Crapper, let me come straight to the point. Many years ago, 1861 to be precise – the year, I understand, that you started your business – my dear father died. His death was a tragedy, the result of an outbreak of typhoid fever at Windsor Castle. The water supply there had become contaminated with the deadly germs. It was only through good fortune that my mother, Her Majesty, was not also smitten. Some ten years later, when I was at Sandringham, I, too,

Thomas meets the Prince of Wales at Buckingham Palace

became extremely ill and almost died from typhus. My family needs to be protected. They must have the highest standards of sanitation – clean water, decent drains, flushing conveniences…'

They were interrupted by a light tap on the door. A maid entered carrying a tray with a silver tea service and a plate of sandwiches which she placed on a side table. She curtseyed and left. Presumably the refreshments were for both of them. But who poured the tea, Thomas wondered? What was the proper etiquette? Normally, a host would pour. But he surely could not expect His Royal Highness to pour for him! Thomas was terrified in case he should do the wrong thing.

The Prince stepped forward. 'Would you please pour, Mr Crapper!' He gestured to the table. 'Everything is for you!'

Thomas noticed that there was only one cup on the tray. He felt nervous.

As he poured from the silver teapot, his hand shook. A great cloud of steam rose from the pot. He lifted the cup to his mouth but it was so hot when it touched his lips that he had to put it down again immediately, spilling tea into the saucer.

Silence. He felt so embarrassed that he dare not look at the Prince. What must he be thinking? Would he excuse Thomas's behaviour as nerves? Or would he think, heaven forbid, that a man who was this clumsy could hardly be trusted with a major project for the royal family?

Thomas felt compelled to fill the silence. 'I'm sorry, Sir.'

The Prince of Wales smiled. 'Tut tut, Mr Crapper. Someone in your line of work with such an unsteady hand, spilling things?' It was clear from his tone that he was only joking but Thomas could not stop himself from turning bright red.

'Let us return to why you are here, Mr Crapper. I have recently received a report on the sanitation at my home at Sandringham in Norfolk. I tell you, it makes depressing reading, all forty-two pages. I cannot have the ghastly events of 1861 repeating themselves, Mr Crapper. I need drains and flushing conveniences, the latest feats of engineering, the best that money can buy. I have seen for myself the power that can be harnessed by water. I saw it at the Niagara Falls some years ago, and I have seen it in Mr Bazelgette's sewers in London.'

'My company could do the work, Sir.'

'Mr Crapper, I haven't said that I am giving you the job yet! Certainly, when I happened to ask my advisers and friends to recommend a respectable company to take on the project, the name of your company kept being mentioned. But it would be a big undertaking. What size is your workforce?'

'Sir, I have ten men working for me, all very experienced.'

'Only ten? You will need more than that. How many could you muster, Mr Crapper?'

'I shall employ as many extra men as we need, sir.'

'I shall need the work finished by the end of November, mind, well in time for Christmas. My family always spends Christmas at Sandringham. And this year, as you know, is a special one for my mother. She has been Queen for fifty years. I am hoping that she will be able to visit. Would you be able to complete the job by this time?'

'I would indeed, sir. You have my word for it!'

The Prince of Wales smiled. 'Very well. My mind is made up. You shall be given the contract. I shall see that it is drawn up. My secretary will be in touch with you.' Then his smile dropped but only for a moment. 'A steady hand though, Mr Crapper. A steady hand!'

Thomas was over the moon. His mouth was dry. It was as much as he could do to thank the Prince. If only his mother could see him now. How proud she would be. What this contract could mean for his business. He would be able to display the royal crest over the entrance to his works in Chelsea. Passers-by would read the prestigious words 'By Appointment to the Royal Family,' or something similar. And if he played his cards right, other royal contracts might come his way. His imagination started to run wild. The name of Thomas Crapper would become famous, not just in Britain but throughout the British Empire – in India, Australia and Canada!

Chapter 2

Many years before, the Prince of Wales's father, Prince Albert, had had flushing toilets installed at the Great Exhibition which opened in Hyde Park in May 1851 to celebrate the marvels of science. Thomas's older brother, George, had visited the Exhibition and delighted in telling Thomas all about it. The greatest attraction was the steam engines: there were almost sixty on view. There was also a watch the size of a tomato pip, and a bed that tipped you out in the morning. As for the toilets, they were amazing.

For many people it was their first experience of a water closet. There were supposed to be sixty-nine of them altogether, designed by George Jennings.

'And they weren't even called water closets but *halting stations.*'

Thomas laughed. 'Halting stations!'

'Yes, and you had to pay to use them. People expected the cost to be included in the entrance charge for the Exhibition. How wrong they were. You had to pay the attendant a halfpenny to use the ones in the refreshment rooms and spend a whole penny to use the ones in the main hall.'

'And did many people use them?' asked Thomas.

'Why, yes,' said George. 'Think of all those visitors who had made a long journey by train or bus. They were bursting when they arrived, and headed straight for the water closets. Apparently, they made a great profit, and the man who was responsible for looking after them and collecting the coins received a medal for his services.'

But having a W.C. in one's home was unusual. Those who did own one had it situated as an extension at the back of the house, or under the stairs, or in a partitioned area of the bedroom. To avoid an awful smell you needed to have a toilet with an 'S' bend or 'stink trap'.

The majority of homes in the country did not have a W.C. even if they could have afforded one. Chamber pots (known as 'piss pots') and commodes were acceptable because they were generally (apart from in the case of invalids), used only for urine. Many people shuddered to think about the idea of sitting on a lavatory inside the house and emptying your bowels. It would call for a major change in public attitude to make this acceptable. And so they carried on using garden privies. The sewage from garden privies and chamber pots was then emptied into cesspools which built up for years until eventually 'night soil men' took the mess away in carts. Often they just dumped it into streams and rivers. From these same streams and rivers Londoners drew their water for washing and cooking – 'wriggly water' because of all the bacteria in it.

As a result of all this, it was scarcely surprising that the city was a desperately unhealthy place. Everything about London stunk. There was the sweet, sickly stink of cesspools and sewers; the sharp stink of rotting rubbish; the acrid stink of smoke rising from the chimneys of houses and factories. Thomas would have been used to all these odours.

Living conditions were bad enough in the west of the city where his brother lived. Many houses had to rely on street water pumps that were turned on for just a few hours each day. Only the main streets had sewers, and these often got clogged up. But in the East End of London, especially around Whitechapel, Hackney and Bethnal Green, conditions were very much worse. Houses were built so close together that the air was rank, germs thrived and respiratory diseases such as bronchitis and consumption (tuberculosis) were rife.

The 'night soil men' emptying the cesspools

Five years before Thomas arrived in London the city authorities had been given the power to set up boards of health. These boards were made up of important local men who were responsible for the sewerage and drainage, and the cleaning of the streets. But the problem was that unless the death rate was exceptionally high, or enough rate payers demanded improvements, nothing much was done. Besides, many people did not like the government interfering in affairs that they believed were none of its business.

As the population rose, the problems of disposal grew worse and one of London's rivers, the Fleet, became a fermenting open sewer. No one at this time was aware of the dangers of polluted water, and it was only in the 1850s that Dr John Snow proved that disease could be spread by microbes in water. Unfortunately, by then, thousands of Londoners had died from drinking water that had become polluted by the excrement of victims of the deadly cholera and typhoid diseases. The statistics are horrifying: the average age of death in Bethnal Green in East London was forty-five for a gentleman; twenty-six for a tradesman; and just sixteen for a labourer.

This, then, was the grim world into which Thomas Crapper was born, and this was the London into which he ventured.

Chapter 3

Thomas Crapper was born in 1836 in the hamlet of Waterside in south Yorkshire. The nearest town was Thorne, which lay about a mile to the south, on the road to Doncaster. Thorne was a thriving little town of just over 4,000 inhabitants, with a weekly Wednesday market, two annual fairs and plans to install gas lighting before the year was out.

The Crappers lived in a cottage next to one of the boatyards on the banks of the River Don. Most of these Waterside cottages were tiny, and some of the present houses are two of the original cottages combined. (The soprano Lesley Garrett spent her childhood at No.9). But when Thomas was a boy anything up to nine inhabitants might be crammed inside a cottage. Their livelihoods were mostly connected with the River Don or the canal which linked Thorne to the River Trent – many of the men being watermen, sail-makers, ships' carpenters or rope-makers. Next door to the Crappers, at No.77, lived the Wharams. The father, Joseph Wharam, was a ship owner's clerk and he encouraged his sons to follow in his footsteps by learning accounts and book keeping. As we shall see, his younger son, Robert Marr Wharam, was to play a crucial part in Thomas's later life.

Crapper was a traditional Yorkshire name: originally it was Cropper – someone who brings in the crops. But for many years now the family's livelihood had been connected not with farming but with the water. Thomas's father, Charles, a man with a wide face, bulging eyes and long side-whiskers, was the captain of one of the new steamships, a small paddle steamer called the *Aquabus,* which berthed with large sailing vessels at the quay. The vessel operated daily, at half past eight each morning, taking passengers to Hull where they boarded larger vessels to sail down the coast to London.

His mother, Sarah Crapper, ran the house. She was a small woman, though her bonnet and billowing sleeves made her appear bigger than she really was. Thomas could remember hearing her argue with his father over money. Charles Crapper did not bring home much money, so, to make ends meet, the family took in lodgers – an apprentice bookkeeper and, later on, two stewardesses who worked on the ships. This made the house too crowded for Thomas, who preferred walks in the fresh air. Sometimes he would meet up with his cousin, Maria Green. (Maria pronounced her name Mariah, like the American singer and song writer Mariah Carey). He liked Maria, she made him laugh, and they would go on walks together along the riverbank. She had a weak chest, and her parents thought that the fresh air would do her good.

Thomas had seven brothers. The first born, George, had moved to London where he was a plumber; Charles and John had also left home; and Robert, James and Henry worked as dockers in the shipbuilding yards. There was also William, who was three years younger than Thomas.

For his brothers, the working day never varied. They helped in the yards, tied up boats at the wharf, and loaded and unloaded cargo. Although they might call themselves 'dockers', they were more like casual labourers who were paid only for the hours they worked. Sometimes there was nothing for them to do, and they would just have to hang around on the quay waiting for work.

As Thomas walked to school each morning with his brother, William, he often wondered what the future might hold for him. Surely there had to be more in life than what his brothers did. He would make sure of it. His school, the Brooke's Trust School, was a mile

Thorne Quay

away in Thorne. The schoolmaster (the Rev. Eric Rudd, vicar of Thorne, the same man who had baptised him in 1836) seemed to concentrate on teaching Latin to boys who paid fees, rather than boys like Thomas who came from poorer families and were not expected to do well. Most of the time Thomas was with the schoolmaster's deputy, who taught him to read and write, and do a little arithmetic.

By the time that Thomas left the school at fourteen, Waterside had started to change. When his father had become a captain, many years earlier, his ship had been the only one which sailed from the quay. But by the early 1850s other steamships and the first railways were beginning to compete with them. The boatyards were much less busy than when he was a young boy, fewer ships were being built and fewer jobs depended on the water. Their next door neighbour, James Wharam, moved his family away and found employment in nearby Rotherham, where he worked as an agent for shipping and the new railway.

So, even if Thomas had been interested, it was unlikely that there would be work for him in the boatyards in Thorne. But Thomas had dreams of making a name for himself as a young man, of travelling to London, just as his brother George had done. He knew that good money could be made in the plumbing trade because his Uncle James was a plumber and glazier, and owned four cottages in Hatfield, close to Thorne. Just imagine how much more money he could make in London, city of opportunity.

He hoped that his parents would be proud to have a son with ambition. However, when he told his mother his plans she looked unhappy. Although she had herself moved to Yorkshire from Suffolk, she had been settled now for many years with her brood of children. She had already lost George, who had left home and was now working in London. Surely she was not going to lose another son.

'What will you do in London?' she asked.

'I shall train as a plumber...'

'But you could be a plumber here in Thorne, or in Hatfield!'

'Mother, George says that I can make a far better living in London. What with all the people there, they are crying out for plumbers...'

'There is plenty of work *here*. Pipes burst, drains get blocked, cesspools need emptying, if that's the kind of work you have in mind.'

'But George gets work in the houses of rich people, putting in china basins and lavatory pans.'

'Rich people indeed!' said his father, puffing out his chest. 'You mean those that are born with money and have never had to do a day's work. What about us honest hardworking folk in these parts? Your life is *here.*' His eyes seemed to protrude even more than usual. 'The Crappers have lived in Yorkshire for hundreds of years. Our business is the river. And let me tell you straight, lad, that river is the River Don, not the River Thames. And that's an end to it!'

Chapter 4

But Thomas stood firm, and by 1853 he had left home and was living in London where his brother, George, took him on as an apprentice plumber. Tradition has it that he walked to London (a distance of 165 miles) but it is much more likely that his brother paid his boat fare.

George lived in Robert Street, Chelsea; he was a master at his trade and already had several men working for him. As more and more people were installing piped water into their homes there was a greater demand for plumbers to repair their systems, and he was looking for an apprentice. They both signed their names to a huge document, called an indenture because it had a jagged edge like a mouth of teeth. Thomas was committed to stay for seven years with his brother George and his wife, and their young son, another George. During this time he would receive training and be provided with food, drink and accommodation. He would also be paid a wage of four shillings a week, a modest sum but he did have his food and lodging provided. At the end of the seven years, when Thomas would be twenty-one years old, he would be a qualified plumber, an independent man.

His brother's house lay in a terrace of Georgian brick houses in a fashionable district of Chelsea with squares and terraces, sash windows and black iron railings shaped like spears. Steps led up to the front door, above which was a fan-shaped window that cast a beam of light into the hallway; more steps led down to the basement where the kitchen and scullery were situated. Once inside, the staircase was steep and Thomas needed to climb several storeys, passing the half-open doors of a dining room, a drawing room and various bedrooms, before he reached the small servant's room he had been allocated in the attic.

Nearby lived famous residents: the American-born artist, James McNeill Whistler; the playwright, Oscar Wilde; the writers, George Eliot and Mark Twain; the painter, J.M.W.Turner, and one of the Prince of Wales's mistresses, the actress, Lily Langtry.

Along the King's Road were plant nurseries and perfumery gardens. A flower show was held each summer, and there would be music and dancing in the recreation ground with its coloured lamps and fountain. Lying on his bed in his attic room, Thomas dreamed that one day he, too, would have a nursery, a wonderful garden and greenhouses of his own.

A tiny window in his room provided some ventilation and a glimpse of London sky. Over his head an animal of some kind, maybe a bird or a squirrel, could be heard scrabbling around in the eaves; while in the house next door he could clearly hear the voices of children playing. From below, where there was a stove and a cracking fire, wafted up the smell of delicious hot food, stews and roasts. But there was not as much as a fireplace where he was. Although during the winter his brother let him take up a hot brick wrapped in a flannel to put in his bed, his room remained bitterly cold.

But what did he care! He felt sure that he had made the right decision by coming to London. Back in Yorkshire, work on the River Don was becoming ever scarcer, and his father lost his job as captain of the *Aquabus*. Desperate not to let his family down, he had taken on the management of a run down pub on Thorne Quay, called the *Rodney Arms*. But within a year, worn out with worry and sickness, he died.

For Thomas, meanwhile, his father's fears had not been realised and the future looked bright. Each morning he woke at six o'clock to the sound of tradesmen's barrows being dragged along the cobbles in the street below, the hooves of horses pulling the trams, and boys shovelling up horse dung. By seven o'clock he was out at work with his brother, watching him mend pipes that had cracked or taps that were dripping. After a while he was expected to do some of the jobs himself, to clear out blocked drains and hold pipes while George used spanners to tighten nuts. He found that the cold water leaking out of the pipes caused his hands to become chapped and covered with chilblains. But that was no more than a minor inconvenience compared with the dangers of life in London. The constant exposure to typhus and cholera bacteria led to the deaths of hundreds of people at devastating speed in a city that was the most densely populated on earth.

There were also highly dangerous gases. One foggy winter afternoon George asked him to call at a house close by in Kensington. The family living there had complained about the terrible smell coming from the drains. When Thomas arrived a servant took him down to the basement. As he approached, a sour mixture hit his nostrils; and once he had unlatched the door the stench was so unbearable that he had to hold his breath.

It was already getting dark and all he could make out was the faint outline of a panelled-in toilet called a valve closet – often referred to as a 'Thunderbox.' He could not see the soil pipe at all. So he asked the servant to bring him a candle. Shielding the naked flame with the palm of his hand, he grappled behind the pan and felt for the pipe. As he moved his hand along it he felt a break. Possibly the pipe had fractured in the cold. The fumes from the sewage were now overwhelming. Perhaps foolishly, he rested his candle on the ground close to the pipe so as to examine it more carefully.

No sooner than he had done so, there was a terrific explosion which swept Thomas off his feet and threw him to the ground. He fell backwards, hitting his head with a dull thud on a heavy iron water tank. He thought 'that was it!' Everything went dark.

The next thing he knew was being helped to his feet by the servant. Although he felt dazed and confused, he was lucky. He only suffered mild concussion and a sore head. It was nothing that a week in bed, with plenty of warm bricks, could not put right.

If only he had realised that the fumes from the sewage were likely to explode when in contact with a flame. Surely, he thought, there must be a way of ventilating house drains more effectively than this, if only to cut down on the smell, let alone the explosions. If he could come up with a solution, just think how famous and wealthy he would be!

Chapter 5

June 1858

It was barely light when Thomas woke with a start. There was a commotion in the street below. Cries of 'Look out!' and 'Mind yourself mister.' These would have been odd enough at such an early hour on a working day. But today was surely a Sunday. So what on earth was going on?

He leapt out of bed and tore down the stairs. But there was no mistaking it. At the bottom of the road where Robert Street joined King's Road he could see carriage after carriage racing by. Was there a special service in one of the city churches, St Paul's perhaps? But then the oddest thing of all about it struck him. These carriages were not heading towards the city. They were leaving it, and leaving it as fast as they could. He wondered whether there had perhaps been a big fire.

'Hey, where's everyone going?' Thomas called out

to a lad who was shovelling up horse manure from the road.

'As far away as possible, if they've got any sense. Away from the smell.'

'Smell. What smell?' asked Thomas. London always smelt. You just got used to it.

'The river. Haven't you smelt the river? It reeks, mate!'

'Never known it not to!'

'I'm not kiddin' yer. Plague of giant flies someone says they've seen down Battersea way.'

'Load of baloney!'

'Didn't you hear about the Queen? Her and Prince Albert? Only been sailing for a few minutes on the royal barge they had, when they couldn't take the smell no longer and were forced back to land.'

'So why do you stay in London? You could take your shovel some place else. There's always horses around.'

'Move?' It's all right for the toffs – they can afford to leave. Muckrakers like me can't. We'll just have to hold our breath and hope.'

Even at the best of times the river was like a dustbin for rotten food, decaying dogs and cats, and the remains from slaughter houses, tanneries, and dye-works. Robert Street, where Thomas lived, was

Queen Victoria and Prince Albert overcome by the smell
of the Thames

situated a few streets back from the Thames, so Thomas had not noticed that the smell was any worse than usual.

But it must have been worse. London's sewers just could not cope with all the W.C.s being flushed. These sewers had only been designed to collect rainwater, and to discharge it into streams that flowed to the Thames. But during the last few years about 250 tons of sewage was being discharged day in, day out, into the river from these toilets. Most of this sewage remained in London instead of flowing out to sea. Much of it was washed up along the riverside on mudflats where the stench of rotting sewage was so unbearable that you had to clamp a handkerchief over your nose if you were to avoid being overcome by fumes.

By the end of June the rich had had enough. The month was dry, very dry. So dry, that the current of the Thames slowed almost to a stop. It was also hot. So hot, that the sewage floating on the surface began to ferment into a thick scum that gave off a vile stench.

Most people at this time still believed that illnesses and diseases were caused by inhaling bad air or gases (miasmas) arising from things that were going bad. One great miasma, or thick grey fog, seemed to hang over the city most of the time. Although Dr John Snow had shown that cholera was caused by contaminated water, few believed him. Most people thought that the overpowering smell in the air was going to kill them. So the sanitary engineers of the day dumped tons of chemicals into the Thames in order to neutralise the smell. Chloride of lime, chalk lime, slaked lime, and carbolic acid were all thrown in by the ton. The inhabitants of London sat back and waited but none of it did any good.

Before long the smell became so bad that MPs could not sit on the river side of the Houses of Parliament at all. They tried to hang sheets dipped in chloride of lime against the windows but they were useless, and Parliament had to finish early for the summer in 1858, a year that has gone down in history as the 'Year of the Great Stink'.

Here was Thomas in London, over half way through his apprenticeship. He would soon be able to set himself up in business on his own, and there would surely be plenty of work. But, as he stood on Chelsea Bridge looking down at the turgid pale brown water, he began to wonder whether he had made the right move in coming to the capital. How could a country that prided itself on its inventions and was respected throughout the world, have such dreadful sanitation –

not even fit for beasts? Was London going to be the city of opportunity after all; or, was it going to be a huge disappointment?

Chapter 6

After a fortnight of misery and distress, the heat finally broke and the rain came. The Thames began to flow again. The stink began to ease. The rich began to return. And Thomas carried on with his apprenticeship. It was easy for him to live economically because his brother supplied him with food, accommodation and a bag of tools. He was able to save, so that one day he would be able to set himself up in business on his own.

In 1859, after a short illness, his mother suddenly died at home in Yorkshire. The two brothers wanted to return but they just could not leave their work immediately. So Thomas was sent scurrying around to see customers who needed their help urgently, and to apologise to others who would have to wait until they got back from Yorkshire. The funeral, which took place at St Nicholas's Church in Thorne, was well attended, particularly by all his mother's nieces and nephews. For several days afterwards the family was reunited as George and Thomas cleared out the house and sorted through their mother's possessions. It was over a week before they returned to London.

Having completed his apprenticeship, in 1861 Thomas left his brother and set up his own business as a plumber at Marlboro' Cottages in Chelsea. There he combined his skills as a plumber with the art of 'brass finishing,' or polishing brass goods. These goods included brass clips for clamping water pipes to the wall, and, of course, taps, plug holes and gas light fittings.

As he became more confident and prosperous, he realized that he was now able to support a wife. He had kept in touch by letter with his childhood sweetheart, his cousin, Maria Green. He remembered the walks along the river they had taken; how she was not strong, and they had had to pause frequently for her to rest. Two years before, Thomas had seen her again at his mother's funeral and they had renewed their friendship. Maria was exactly the same age as Thomas, just as his own parents had been when they married. After a brief courtship by letter he asked Maria to be his wife.

Thomas waited eagerly for an answer. Usually Maria replied by return of post; but no reply came. Maria needed time to think. A move would mean giving up her life in Thorne which, though dull, was at least secure. To her, London was the other side of the world. But, more important, what were her feelings about Thomas? If she agreed to marry him she would be promising to spend the rest of her life with him. If she refused him she would never see him again. The decision could not be taken lightly. But within a month she had made up her mind and had arrived in London to join him.

At midday on Thursday, 26th July 1860, Thomas and Maria were married in a simple ceremony, attended by a few friends, at Holy Trinity Church in Sloane Street, Upper Chelsea. Sadly, her parents were too infirm to make the journey from Norfolk but sent them their love and best wishes. How happy and proud Thomas felt on that day. Maria had chosen him, she had made the decision to say goodbye to her friends and relatives in Thorne so as to be with him, Thomas Crapper. What a picture of loveliness she was in her ivory gown and lace bonnet. Thomas produced the wedding ring, his mother's own ring that his father had given her on their wedding day, and placed it on Maria's finger. The vicar declared them man and wife, and gave Thomas permission to kiss Maria. As they walked down the aisle the organ thundered in the background, and as they emerged from the church their friends smiled broadly and applauded them.

After the service they went back to the house for their wedding 'breakfast' – stewed oysters, cold game and wedding cake. Their friends raised glasses of sweet white wine, and offered a toast to the happy couple. That afternoon they started on their honeymoon, or 'tour,' as it was called in those days. They had decided to spend a week at the seaside resort of Brighton in Sussex. This south coast town had become so fashionable that it was known as 'the Queen of watering-places,' with its bathing machines and many bath houses. There was plenty to do and see. Apart from a museum and a library, there were two theatres, an opera house and assembly rooms where guests could sip tea, play cards and dance.

The couple stayed in a terraced house in a street set back from the sea. They were provided with breakfast and a meal in the evening; Maria loved her food and the fresh air gave her a keener appetite than ever. Here they spent a lovely week with fine warm weather. They took walks along the sea front and up and down the Chain Pier. They visited the theatre and the spectacular Royal Pavilion which looked just like an

Indian palace. The week passed very quickly, and soon they had to return to London, where Thomas had a business to attend to and Maria had a house to look after.

In the first year of their marriage Maria became pregnant. Thomas hoped that they would have a son who would one day be able to carry on the family business: Thomas Crapper & Son of Chelsea. That way, all Thomas's hard work would not have been in vain. They would name him John Green Crapper. Green was Maria's maiden name.

'I shall make a lace bonnet and knit some little booties,' said Maria.

'And I shall build a cradle for him,' said Thomas.

'You keep saying *him*, but our baby might be a girl.'

'I know. But in time we shall have a boy!'

As it turned out, Thomas was right.

However, from the moment the baby was born it was all too clear that something was dreadfully wrong. John Green Crapper was a very sickly child. His arms and legs stayed abnormally thin while his stomach was swollen. He struggled on, through the harsh winter of 1861, gradually wasting away until, soon after his first birthday, he died. On his death certificate the registrar recorded 'Disease of Mesenteric Gland. Atrophy.' It is possible that he had tuberculosis of the adrenal glands, which are responsible for producing hormones. This would have caused these important glands to shrink, with catastrophic results. Another possibility is that little John had coeliac disease which is caused by a bad reaction to gluten in wheat. Victorians often fed their babies a mixture of flour and milk, and this might have triggered the condition, which is well understood nowadays but would have caused gradual malnourishment and death then.

At this time, half of all children died before reaching five years old, so that little coffins were a familiar sight. They were always white to represent innocence, a life taken away before its time. Poor John's white coffin gleamed in the April sunshine as it was taken down from the hearse by a solitary pall bearer who cradled it in his white gloves. The horses had been trained to keep absolutely still, and only their white plumes stirred in the gentle breeze. Maria, Thomas and his brother George entered Holy Trinity Church for the funeral service, the same church in which little John's parents had been married two summers previously. How happy the couple had been then; how desperate they felt today.

Many parents regularly weathered the deaths of a baby or two, and managed to keep up their spirits by quickly conceiving another child. But for Thomas and Maria it was different. To them it was a terrible blow. As yet, John was their only child and they found it impossible to continue with their daily routines. For the next year both stayed in deep mourning, dressing in black. The loss of his son was to haunt Thomas for the rest of his days.

He was forced to carry on as best he could; somehow the business needed to be kept going. It seemed odd that when his family life had been affected by tragedy, his firm was prospering and that he had more customers than ever before. This was because the population of London was rocketing. The area in which he lived, Chelsea, had become much more congested. Down by the river the wharves were now crowded with courts and alleys, swarming with a mass of very small houses and shops. The air was dirtier than ever, pungent with the acrid smoke belched from chimneys. Meanwhile, beneath the streets, a new sound, a distant rumble, signalled the passing of steam locomotives on the new Metropolitan Underground railway as they hauled carriages full of passengers from Paddington into the City of London, the business centre of the capital.

Other tunnels were also being built. After much persuading, the government had finally granted the engineer, Joseph Bazelgette, £3 million (a vast amount of money in those days) to replace the filthy underground rivers with new sewers. Bazelgette had a vision of a vast subterranean world with sewers that would connect homes to a treatment works where the sewage could be made harmless and pumped far out to sea.

As a result of these developments, more and more people began to have flushing lavatories, and it quickly proved to be a boom period, a golden age, for plumbers. Thomas found himself inundated with work – anything from replacing washers on leaky taps to installing baths and toilet cisterns. This did something to help distract his thoughts from his personal tragedy. But there were many dark moments, especially in the winter months when he would find himself dwelling on what might have been. Sometimes John would appear in his dreams. Then he would wake up in the morning even more distressed. If he had survived, his son would now have been five years old. Thomas would be showing him around the works, he could imagine his little eyes shining with wonder. The loss affected Maria differently. She managed to put aside the past but she was terrified of giving birth to another poor little creature like John.

Thomas was now employing a staff of ten workers, including some very promising apprentices, one of whom was his nephew George, the son of his brother who had set Thomas up in London and had given him such a good start. He now had a chance to show his gratitude.

As much as Thomas loved his business, he hated paper work because it took him away from tinkering around with his cisterns and drains. But he was also aware how important it was to any successful business for careful accounts to be kept, money banked and bills paid on time. For this he needed a business partner. He chose Robert Marr Wharam, a man eighteen years his junior. Wharam's parents had lived next door to the Crappers in Thorne when he was growing up and had since moved to London where they had bought a house in Kensington, not far from Thomas's works. They were very much aware that both Thomas and his older brother, George, had been highly successful in London, having both become masters in their business.

Joseph Wharam happened to write Thomas a letter, recommending his son to him, at the very time when Thomas was looking for someone to manage his office.

A commercial clerk by training, Robert Marr Wharam would be just the man to bring his financial and accounting skills to the business. He brought with him to his interview several pages copied from account ledgers, and Thomas was impressed by his methodical layout and immaculate copperplate handwriting. Strangely, although the day was hot and there was scarcely a cloud in the sky, Wharam had also brought with him an umbrella! He tried to put Wharam at his ease but he remained stiff and serious. Thomas put it down to nerves. That the person sitting in front of him should come from his own birthplace and his family had been neighbours to his own dear parents convinced him that he should give him a job. In Robert Marr Wharam he thought he would have a hard working and dedicated business partner who would prove to be a great asset.

But Wharam was to remain stiff and serious. He was such a pessimist that he continued to carry an umbrella with him at all times, forever expecting rain. Wharam was also a deeply religious man who could not tolerate people who smoked or drank. The workers thought that he looked down his nose at them and did not like him at all. They were used to Thomas's gentleness and kind-hearted ways.

Over the years, Robert Marr Wharam managed to

prove himself much more than just an office manager. He accumulated considerable theoretical engineering expertise and even wrote a short book giving advice to house owners about drains and ventilation, so as to stop their house becoming what he called a 'death trap.'

In 1866 Thomas's firm moved to larger premises, a two-storey building which occupied No.s 50, 52 and 54 Marlborough Road (now Draycott Avenue). Business had never been so good. Thomas was no longer merely a plumber: he could now call himself a 'sanitary engineer.'

Chapter 7

Thursday, 18th October 1866. 10 a.m. The whole team of workers crowded around the panel as Thomas Crapper stood ready to start the test. But Robert Wharam did not come to watch: he said he had some 'paperwork' to see to. The men were relieved to hear it because they could relax and be themselves.

The test should have been completed several days before. But it had to be rescheduled. First there had been problems securing the hold-down bolts on No. 4. Then No. 3 had malfunctioned. But all now seemed ready. Thomas took out his watch and tapped the glass. Just over one minute to go. He stroked his neat beard. His hazel eyes twinkled as he looked along the row of workmen – strong, reliable men who took pride in their work and looked forward to days such as this one when they were testing something out.

Thomas had assembled a test panel of five toilets on the ground floor of his cistern workshop. Each cistern was named after one of the streets close to his works – streets with expensive houses: the *Marlboro'*, the *Walton*, the *Ovington*, the *Cadogan* and the *Sloane*. Each one had to make an efficient flush. A massive cast iron tank, holding 200 gallons of water, stood ready on the roof to flush them.

As it would have been most improper and undignified to get someone to sit on each toilet and flush real human sewage, conditions had to be simulated. Instead of 'soil', the workers had prepared a variety of other items such as sponges, cotton waste, grease, and crumpled up pieces of paper which they called 'air vessels.' All these were now bobbing around in the water, ready for the big event.

The men gathered around with furrowed brows. It was their most ambitious test yet. The room crackled with tension. Total silence in the workshop. Outside, in the yard they briefly heard the sound of horses' hooves on the cobbles as the delivery cart returned from a run. The reputation of the company depended upon the success of its cisterns. Perhaps this time they would fail. But its owner, chain-pull in hand, and poised for the big test, was brimming with confidence. His men had worked hard getting everything ready and, as a reward, they would all be getting beer with their lunch today. As for Mr Wharam, a teetotaller, tucked away in his office, he would be none the wiser.

Thomas studied his pocket watch and gave it another tap. Ten seconds to go. There was a countdown. At five seconds one of the men stifled a cough. His boss raised an eyebrow in half-hearted reproof. Then Thomas pulled the chain of No. 1, the *Marlboro'*. Everyone heard the down-rush of water into the pan, the gurgle at the end of the flush; the hissing sound of the water coming in to refill the

A disastrous toilet test

cistern. A brief round of applause. The *Walton* and*Ovington* also performed well. Thomas beamed.

The chain was pulled on the No.4 cistern, the *Cadogan.* But nothing happened. Thomas pulled the chain again, this time with more force. Still nothing. Suddenly there was a grating sound. Everyone stepped back. The valve had separated from its moorings.

'Oh Lord!' said Thomas. 'It's those bolts again!'

Water started to splash down on everybody below. Then the entire cistern overbalanced and came crashing to the floor. The men looked across at their employer with looks of horror on their faces. But Thomas just stood there, stroking his beard and giving one of his rueful smiles:

'Nothing that can't be put right. At least Her Majesty the Queen wasn't standing underneath!'

Chapter 8

Thomas Crapper's pride and joy was not so much his cistern workshop but his showrooms, the first bathroom showrooms in the world. Thomas had a great sense of fun and used shock tactics to promote himself and his firm to a wary public. He had knocked out the sash windows from the ground floor in Marlborough Road and had installed large shop windows. Originally he had only displayed 'Thunderboxes' in the showrooms; but by the early 1880s he was displaying the new, free-standing, decorated ceramic lavatory pans. Thomas invited the public inside to view all the products and even to try them, as many of the W.C.s, basins and baths were plumbed in. Previously, if you wished to order sanitary ware, a salesman discretely visited your home with a catalogue of engravings (usually in black and white) and a handful of samples or models, each only a few inches high. From these items and the salesman's advice you had to choose the contents of your bathroom. Now, full-size working sanitary ware was prominently on display. Thomas was determined to persuade Londoners that there was nothing shameful about wanting to examine and try out these fixtures.

Behind the showrooms, an archway led through to the yard and the brass foundry where pipes and clips, taps and chains were manufactured. His workers – by this time there were twelve men and twelve boys – checked and tested every item before it left the works, and should any part not come up to standard, it would be taken to Thomas's repairs workshop next to the foundry.

The business soon became famous for its quality workmanship, attention to detail and excellent customer service, and Thomas prospered. As a result, he moved up the social ladder, he could now call himself 'middle class,' and could afford to live in the London suburbs. There he would find a larger house; then they might consider employing a servant who lived in – because members of the middle class did that sort of thing.

And so, in 1867, they left Robert Street and moved in to No. 1, Middleton Road (now Buckmaster Road), S.W.11, close to the wide open spaces of Clapham Common, fringed by elegant houses, and a short walk from Clapham Junction railway station, from where he could take a train to London. This two storey, end of terrace house had no front garden worthy of the name, the house bordering directly on the street. So, to make up for this, Thomas added some window boxes and made a charming rose trellis in front of the door.

Over the next few years, his brother George, who was living close by in Gorst Road, helped him develop No.8 and No.10 opposite – the biggest houses in Middleton Road – and, of course, installed flushing toilets. In 1874 all was ready and Thomas and Maria moved across to No.8. Maria was very pleased with the new house, which had three storeys, and plenty of light pouring through its tall sash windows and ground floor bow window. They also now had a large back garden. The couple had really come up in the world, and their house reflected this improved status. Maria enjoyed her new life, particularly selecting the menus and discussing the meals with the cook. That was her main interest!

But, for Thomas, personal happiness did not come with that status. Unlike his brother George, Thomas still had no children. He wished he could hear the peal of children's laughter in his new house, of them racing up and down the stairs, playing games in his lovely big garden. He wanted a son, a boy similar to George's, a keen lad who was learning fast. But as each year passed, no more children were born; nor were they likely to be born because Maria was approaching forty. Before long, Thomas began to give up hope and instead threw himself headlong into his business.

Chapter 9

Certainly there was plenty of work for Thomas. Toilets at this time were often poorly designed. They had a tank of water overhead with a pull chain attached to a plug-stopper or 'valve.' When you pulled the chain the plug was plucked out and the cistern flushed the pan. But some people attached weights to the chain, keeping the stopper out and allowing the fresh water entering the cistern to constantly pour out again into the bowl. Even without doing this, many stoppers failed to seal properly when the chain was released, and huge quantities of clean water were wasted. At the very least these toilets needed constant attention from plumbers. At worst they caused floods.

The Metropolis Water Act of 1871 aimed to prevent this terrible waste of water by requiring that manufacturers build into their cisterns a mechanism called a 'water waste preventer.' This is what we now call a syphon and, unlike the old valves, it cannot leak, so no water is ever wasted. From now on, the moment the toilet was flushed, water could not flow again until the cistern had refilled. When the user pulled the chain – or pressed the lever – the whole volume of water in the cistern was released rapidly with a tremendous gush. As it had only one moving part, it proved to be very reliable. It was also very powerful. At the Health Exhibition in London a few years later a 'water waste preventer' succeeded in flushing away, amongst other items, ten apples averaging over one and three-quarter inches each in diameter.

With all this interest in reliable flushing toilets, it was not surprising that Thomas's business continued to expand. He put in a long working day, made longer still by his visits after work to repair cisterns; he would take special delight if it was one of his rival's items of plumbing that had broken.

One evening, he had been out to a customer's home at Streatham in south-east London to interest him in a 'water waste preventer.' He had made a sale and was in a particularly jolly mood. However, as he was returning to Streatham Hill railway station on his way home, he started to shiver. By the time he reached the station he felt feverish and his limbs began to ache, so he went into the waiting room and lay down on a bench. A porter who spotted him through the window assumed he had come across a drunk and went off to fetch the station master. When they returned they found Thomas very groggy indeed. They managed to find his address from an envelope in his pocket and called for a horse and trap to take him back home.

When he arrived at Middleton Road, Maria was so concerned that she fetched the doctor straight away. The diagnosis was not good: like hundreds of others in London, Thomas was suffering from smallpox. Along with typhus and cholera, this was still one of the most feared diseases of the day. There had recently been a smallpox epidemic in England but it seemed to have run its course and Thomas thought he had been spared. But that was not the case. He had smallpox. He had obviously come into contact with a carrier of the disease. If he survived, he would be left with terrible scars all over his body. But perhaps he would never recover. If so, what would happen to his wife? Would she have enough money to live comfortably? She did not have very good health. Who would look after her? And what about his business?

Chapter 10

If Thomas had been born ten or so years later, he might have been given a smallpox vaccine as part of a government scheme introduced in 1853. But by then he was an apprentice in London, working for his brother, and it did not occur to them to get vaccinated. They were too busy fitting pipes and repairing cisterns. Besides, George had heard terrible stories about perfectly fit and healthy people who had been given the smallpox vaccine only to die in agony when a nasty ulcer developed. Maybe it wasn't surprising, he thought, since the vaccine originated from a sick cow. Better just to hope that you never caught smallpox, or, if you were unlucky, that at least you caught it mildly and made a full recovery.

But Thomas had caught a severe strain of the disease. Maria nursed him with great care. Using a pipette, she carefully measured out drops of laudanum to help relieve the pain; and she pressed cold cloths against his face to try to reduce the fever. Every evening she brewed him strong beef tea in an effort to build up his strength.

Fortunately, after three weeks, Thomas began to slowly recover and the scabs started to fall off. The feeling that he had been saved from a horrible death spurred him on and gave him a fresh burst of energy. Thomas was now at his best, his most enterprising, his most inventive.

Over the next few years he took out nine patents for inventions connected with the toilet, or improvements to existing devices. One of his inventions was to improve the 'Disconnecting Trap.' This device broke the connection between the main sewage drains and the ordinary house drain. He solved the terrible problem of sewage choking up the part of the drain known as the inspection chamber by getting deposits of sewage to pass through a narrow, egg-shaped section of pipe. From there it quickly flowed into the main drain, greatly cutting down on the awful sewer smells. The improved 'Disconnecting Trap' became an essential underground drains fitting and was a great leap forward in the campaign against disease.

Three more of Thomas's patents were for W.C.s. One of these had a spring-loaded, self-raising seat which was supposed to leap up when the user got to their feet and flush the bowl automatically. It was an ingenious idea, way ahead of its time. Unfortunately, over time the rubber buffers under the seat became tacky and this made the seat stick to the bowl for a few moments after use. When the seat broke free, it shot up, giving a very nasty surprise slap on the bare bottom. It was not a financial success and quickly got the nickname of 'bottom slapper.'

Thomas also introduced an improved 'Means for

The 'bottom slapper'

Operating the Mechanism of Water Closets,' controlled by a foot lever, rather like we might operate a pedal bin today. Not a single drop of water was wasted because as soon as the foot was removed from the pedal the valve was closed and the water stopped. Apart from making it easier for invalids to use the toilet, it was helpful for emptying slops because both hands were free to hold the bucket.

Apart from the W.C.s themselves, Thomas built silencers which cut down the hissing and gurgling noises that cisterns were prone to make when they were filling up. The most famous of his models to be fitted with a silencer was the *Marlboro' Silent Water Waste Preventer* – named once again after his works in Chelsea. This high level cistern was situated about 6 feet 6 inches above the pan, and could be flushed when the cistern was only two-thirds full. It operated extremely efficiently and lived up to Thomas's catchphrase: 'A certain flush with every pull.'

Most of his designs came with polished mahogany, walnut or oak hinged seats and lids. More and more of his bowls were patterned because it made them attractive to look at, and disguised their true use. Some claim that there were cases of ladies being shocked when they saw the reflections of their bottoms in the plain white pans! Patterning generally made them even

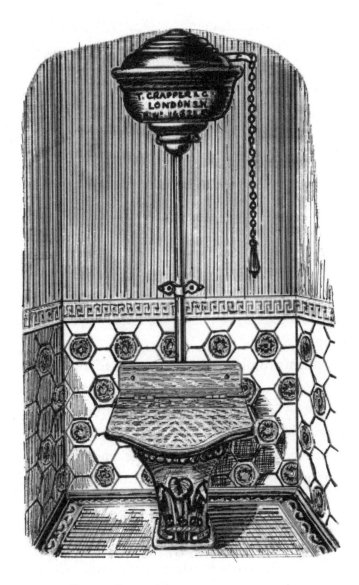

Thomas Crapper's 'water waste preventer'

more expensive, though the *Deluge,* with its lovely floral bowl and cistern, was within the budget of the middle classes.

Thomas was always on the watch out for new ideas. One of his own workers, Albert Giblin, took out a patent for a 'Valveless Water Waste Preventer' (Patent No. 4990). The cistern could be flushed when only half full, whereas most cisterns needed to be completely full. Not only this, but it had very few parts, and those it did have – a spindle and plates – fitted together so snugly that it hardly ever went wrong. Thomas was so impressed that he bought the rights to manufacture the cistern from Giblin. He was then able to market the device himself with his own name on it.

At this time he developed a friendship with Thomas Twyford who had a factory at Hanley, near Stoke-on-Trent, in the Potteries. Twyford, the potter, helped Thomas Crapper with designs for toilet pans; in exchange, Thomas Crapper, the engineer, helped Twyford with his cisterns. So grateful was he that each Christmas Twyford sent three 60lb chests of tea to London – one for Thomas, another for Thomas's nephew George, and the third for Wharam.

All of Thomas's products appeared in the firm's catalogues and came to be installed in public conveniences, hotels, factories and London schools. They included cisterns, iron baths, and sinks for housemaids that were built into cupboards so they would not have to take the slops all the way down to the scullery. There were also speciality products: shower sprays, drinking fountains and heated towel rails. There were 'closet chairs' (a kind of portable toilet); urinals for workhouses and railways; and special toilets without chains for prisons, so that the inmates could not rip them off and use them to attack the guards! There were elaborately decorated beer-pump handles; radiators for churches; even a smoke generating machine for testing the drains. He also designed a special container for toilet paper which could be fixed on the wall next to the lavatory. This was a time when many people felt uncomfortable asking for toilet paper, so it was kept under the counter in shops, and if anyone asked for it, they would refer to it as 'curl paper' instead. ('Curl papers' were originally sheets used for curling women's hair).

Soon the firm of Thomas Crapper was becoming so well known in London, and its catalogues circulated so widely, that orders began to increase. He took out advertisements in national newspapers, all discretely worded of course, and orders began to come in from all over the country. His name even came to be known in royal circles. Thomas was famous.

Chapter 11

On that memorable morning when Thomas was awarded the contract to install the drains and plumbing at Sandringham House he could not believe his good fortune. It was an incredible achievement to win such a prestigious contract. But the Royal Warrant was there in black and white for all to see:

These are to certify that I have appointed
Mr Thomas Crapper, trading under the
Style of T. Crapper and Company, Chelsea
Into the Place and Quality of
Sanitary Engineers to His Royal Highness.
To have, hold, exercise and enjoy the said Place
Together with all Rights, Profits, Privileges and
Advantages thereunto belonging.
This appointment is personal and does not
Extend to any further member of the firm.
And so for doing, this shall be your Warrant.

Thomas, who was by nature a modest man, was tremendously proud. He dreamed of showing the Prince of Wales around Sandringham House when the work was complete. Perhaps the Prince would praise him: 'You have done extremely well here, Mr Crapper!'

The commission gave him the right to display at his Marlboro' works a royal crest painted blue, red and gold, and measuring seven feet by five. Underneath the crest, in three foot-high letters, were inscribed the words: 'By Appointment MANUFACTURING SANITARY ENGINEERS.'

Thomas now had a duty to really impress the Prince. He at once made a preliminary visit to Sandringham, and drew up a list of everything that was needed: at least 30 water closets, Kenwhars (Kensington and Wharam) and Marlboro's, with expensive cedar seats and enclosures. Then there were flushing tanks, disconnecting traps, pipework, manhole covers, baths, basins and showers. As well as the Queen's and Prince of Wales's apartments to provide for, there were the rooms of the ladies-in-waiting, guests and servants. He also had instructions to install flushing urinals next to the billiards room for the players to use. It was quite a list, and on his return to Chelsea he gave instructions for his team to set to work straight away.

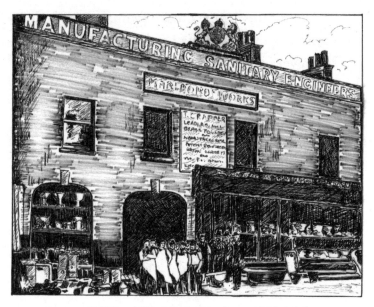
Outside the works

Some weeks later, the Prince of Wales inspected the work to see how all the fittings were progressing. All went very well and the Prince was delighted with what he saw. Thomas's only regret was that when they were alone and the Prince asked him for a light for his cigar he could not help, as he did not smoke. From that day onwards he made a resolution always to carry a box of matches in his pocket.

When everything was ready, the cisterns and bowls were taken up to Sandringham and installed, and sewer pipes and drains connected. Thomas returned to London, imagining that his work was now complete.

However, one morning about a week later, Maria handed him a letter:

'This has just arrived in the post for you, dear.' She was out of breath, having hurried up the stairs. Her look was fixed on the crest at the top of the envelope.

'It's from the Prince of Wales,' said Thomas.

He tore open the envelope, ripping the top of the letter in his haste.

'His private secretary…'

He scanned the page. 'My goodness, Maria. I have been asked to go to Sandringham to demonstrate all our new fittings… and you have been invited to accompany me!'

Maria was stunned into silence for a few moments. Then she gasped. 'Oh dear, I really don't…'

Thomas adjusted his tie. 'Of course you must come!'

Maria looked worried. 'I wouldn't know what to say or do.'

'Don't worry on that account. I'm sure everything will be all right. Just be yourself.'

'But how would I greet the Prince? Surely I would have to curtsey. And I don't have anything to wear.' This was something of an exaggeration as Maria had many dresses in her wardrobe. But the truth was that she had been putting on some weight recently and this occasion gave her the perfect excuse for a new outfit.

'Oh, I'm sure you can practise at home in front of the mirror. It can't be that difficult. And you can have a new outfit. We shall go shopping!'

And so they went shopping to Peter Jones department store in King's Road, Chelsea, close to his Marlboro' works. There, Maria bought a hat trimmed with feathers and ribbons; a pair of long gloves; and was measured for a fur-trimmed jacket, a new dress with wide shoulders and a high lace collar. Thomas made do with a new frock coat and hat.

On a fine autumn day, a fortnight later, they were on their way to Sandringham. They boarded the train at Clapham Junction for the short journey to Victoria, where they took the omnibus to King's Cross station and boarded a Great Eastern Railway train. Carriage doors were slammed shut, and there were shouts to 'stand away.' Shrill whistles. The train jolted to a start and pulled slowly out of the station, with smoke pouring from the funnel of the locomotive. Soon they emerged from the arched roof of the station and into the sunlight. After passing through the north London suburbs they started to gather speed. They made frequent stops at strange sounding places such as

Downham Market and Watlington; the only place name they recognized being Cambridge. As it was such a special day they had ordered a hamper from the famous grocers Fortnum & Mason in Piccadilly. When they opened it they found a game pie, fruit and a bottle of white wine.

Towards the end of the journey the land became very flat, and in the distance the couple thought they could spot the sea. After almost two hours they reached their destination, Wolferton station which had been built especially to serve the Sandringham estate. A fine black carriage with a royal crest on its side was waiting outside the station to take them to Sandringham House, just over two miles away. As they travelled through the open countryside, fallen leaves stretched out in all directions, forming a carpet of russet. In the distance they could see a medieval stone castle with a gateway and towers.

After about a quarter of an hour they caught sight of Sandringham House, a red brick building with turrets and tall chimney stacks built in the Tudor style, as at Hampton Court. Surrounding it were acres of gardens, entered through iron gates. The carriage came to a halt on a gravel driveway where an elderly servant dressed in red livery greeted them and helped them down the steps.

'Please follow me.' They were amazed because he spoke like a gentleman, not a servant.

He escorted them to the house where they were led into a grand entrance hall with a large fireplace, a gallery and many oil paintings. The servant gestured towards some seats covered with red velvet.

'Please make yourselves comfortable.'

There he left them. They looked at each other in amazement. Maria felt nervous and adjusted her jacket. 'Do I look all right?'

Thomas held her hand and reassured her. 'You look fine.'

At that point the door opened and the servant returned. 'Please follow me,' he said, and escorted them down a long corridor to the Prince of Wales's apartments. They entered a rather dark room with ornate wooden panelling and huge windows that looked out on to the gardens. Hanging from the walls were large gilt-edged pictures and the heads of stuffed wild animals, including a tiger and stags. On the floor there was a tiger skin rug. The Prince of Wales stood before them, fatter than ever, dressed in a tweed jacket and with a cigar in his hand. Thomas bowed and Maria curtseyed. He said how pleased he was to see Thomas again, and how glad he was that Maria had been able to come too. The Prince turned to light his cigar. At that point Thomas instinctively patted his waistcoat pocket where he always kept a box of matches.

'Perhaps, Mr Crapper, your wife would like some refreshments while you check over the fittings with our engineer.' He then added with a smile. 'But no slopping, Mr Crapper. No slopping!' So, he had remembered. How embarrassing!

Maria was shown into a cosy sitting room with sofas and a log fire, where the head housekeeper, Mrs Grace, poured tea from a silver teapot into dainty cups. On the table were plates of fruit cake and bread and butter with the crusts cut off. As Maria ate, the housekeeper asked her about her life in London. Just like the servant who had helped them down from their carriage, she too did not speak like a servant but in a refined manner, like a lady.

Within an hour, Thomas was escorted back to the sitting room. He was all smiles: the tour had obviously been successful. Mrs Grace was most apologetic: 'I'm afraid the tea is cold. Would you like me to order some more for you?'

'That is very kind of you but no thank you. We must be on our way, otherwise we shall miss our train back to London.'

She asked whether they would like to use the bathroom before they left. They both said yes. Maria was delighted to see in action all the equipment her husband had installed. And the flush worked! There was also the most fragrant cream soap and the most luxurious soft towels imaginable.

Mrs Grace escorted them both to the front door where they made their farewells. As they walked back to the carriage, Thomas pointed to the manhole cover in the ground nearby, inscribed 'Thomas Crapper. Chelsea.' Maria's eyes shone as she was helped up into the carriage. It had been a wonderful day. She felt like a queen.

Chapter 12

Following this success at Sandringham, Thomas was awarded commissions to provide toilets and bathrooms at other royal residences, including Windsor Castle and Buckingham Palace. Royal approval helped his business to flourish more than ever before. He was also asked to supply the Prince of Wales with an armchair upholstered in velvet that hid a complete flushing lavatory; it was to be installed in Leighton House in West Hampstead, the home of his mistress, Lily Langtry.

In the centre of London at Westminster Abbey there are three manhole covers between the cloisters and West Dean's Yard, about thirty feet from the exit – further evidence of his success.

As his company went from strength to strength, Thomas was able to equip his home with good quality furniture. He was soon doing so well that in 1890 he and Maria moved out of London to Brighton where they had spent their honeymoon almost thirty years earlier. While on holiday in the town the previous summer, they had found a vacant property at No.21 Powis Square. The square was bordered by very elegant three-storey houses with bow fronts and iron balconies situated around a central garden. An added advantage was that it was a select neighbourhood and the residents were likely to be quiet: on one side lived a widow and on the other a clergyman.

Thomas was in extremely good spirits on the morning they moved from Middleton Road to Brighton. For him and Maria it was literally a breath of fresh air. They took with them their two servants, Ellen Sherwood and Lucy Green. For a while they also employed an old cook who used to drink the gin in the sideboard decanter and replace it with water.

With no surviving children of their own, Thomas and Maria loved to have visitors – especially their nieces and nephews. Their great-nephew, Frank, frequently stayed with them, and he thought the old cook was great fun. It was on one such visit that the cook was caught squeezing him into the 'dumb waiter', a small lift for food and plates, and winding him up from the kitchen to the dining room. This was the final straw and they sacked her.

The Crappers were just one of numerous middle class families who had moved out of the capital to make Brighton their home. The town was so close to London, less than fifty miles away, that it was sometimes described as 'the seaside suburb of London.' It became home for many who worked on the Stock Exchange, or at the Bank of England in Threadneedle Street and who, thanks to an efficient railway connection, could be at home in time for a trip out in the horse and trap before dinner. In fact they could reach home almost as quickly as if they had been living at Wandsworth or Kew in South London.

Many of them were not sorry to see the back of London with its crowds, bad smells and protest marches by dockers who were on strike. Then there were those terrible Whitechapel murders a couple of years back. Jack the Ripper had never been caught. Perhaps he had gone into hiding and would reappear in West London, to pluck his next helpless victim from the streets. Far safer to be out of London altogether.

To provide for all the new residents, as well as the seasonal visitors, a huge building programme had taken place since Thomas and Maria had spent their honeymoon there. Few coastal towns at this time could boast so fine a set of hotels – the Grand, the Hotel Metropole, the Bedford, the Norfolk, Prince's. The most impressive of these was the Grand which can still be seen today on the seafront. This was now the age of electricity, and most of these hotels were fitted with electric lighting and electric passenger lifts. Thomas was awestruck, and over the next few months followed suit by introducing electric lighting in his London showrooms. It had the great advantage of being able to illuminate all corners of a room, unlike the old gas lamps which had cast shadows.

As a 'Sanitary Engineer,' Thomas was at the height of his career and could hold his head high in Brighton society. His name appeared in the 'court' section of the local directories, alongside clergymen and gentlemen, rather than amongst the list of tradesmen. Like many other prominent men in the town he joined the local Freemasons, and Maria was sometimes allowed to accompany him to their dinners, which she greatly enjoyed. A photo taken of her at this time shows a full-faced, plump woman in a patterned dress and lace collar. Her hair is drawn up into a bun, which made her look older than she really was, around fifty-five, the same as Thomas.

Each morning Thomas could comfortably walk the journey from his house to the railway station in ten

Thomas and Maria on Brighton seafront

minutes. There he boarded the 7.35 a.m. semi-fast train to Victoria station in London. The journey time was just over one and a half hours. He returned on the 4.30 p.m. express train which arrived back in Brighton at

5.45 p.m. He had purchased an annual season ticket from the London, Brighton and South-Coast Railway and became used to the daily journey.

Robert Wharam and his wife, Amelia, also moved out of London to the south coast at the same time as the Crappers. But rather than move to Brighton, which was becoming rather touristy, they upstaged Thomas and Maria by choosing the higher class resort of Eastbourne, a resort built 'for gentlemen by gentlemen.' Brighton might call itself the 'Queen' of watering places but Eastbourne billed itself as the 'Empress' of watering places and boasted beautiful gardens and electric lights all along the seafront.

This one-upmanship was typical of Wharam who remained as aloof and superior as ever. And it was not just the workers who disliked him; he was also beginning to fall out with Thomas Crapper. The main problem concerned their showrooms – they could not agree about what should be sold there. Right from the start they had sold other firms' products, provided they satisfied Thomas's high standards. Wharam now wanted to start selling brassware made by others and reduce production at their works. This upset Thomas who wanted to keep his own company's considerable range, of which he was so proud. Although he always tried his hardest to remain loyal to his fellow

Yorkshireman in front of his workers, they could sometimes sense the undercurrents of tension between them and hear raised voices coming from the offices.

While the pair of them commuted to London from their separate seaside resorts, a lot of work was being completed on the sanitation system of Brighton. The main problem was the smell of sewage, especially in the summer, and the very poor ventilation of house sewers. In order to improve the situation, sewers were connected up more efficiently and charcoal was used to neutralize the smell coming up from road sewers.

Thomas was delighted with these initiatives. They pointed towards a brighter and healthier future in the town where he and Maria hoped to retire and spend their old age. If only their son was with them to enjoy that future. John Green Crapper would have now been about thirty, an age when Thomas was already a master plumber. He wondered what he might have looked like. Perhaps a smaller version of himself. But sadly it was not to be, and since that time the couple had not been blessed with any more children.

Chapter 13

Now almost sixty years old, Thomas was beginning to tire of the daily journey to London. So, in 1895, he and Maria reluctantly moved back from Brighton to the London suburbs. They had enjoyed the sea air of Brighton and were determined to find a place on high ground where the air was clear and healthy, far away from the city fogs. They chose Anerley, south-east of London, which was being built on the Kent countryside. A local estate agent called the area 'the fresh air suburb' because it caught breezes from the coast. Thomas already knew the area well because he had installed W.C.s and drains in a number of streets there. In Thornsett Road – he was attracted by the name, it sounded so much like his birthplace – he bought a house (No.12) with a large bay window and the back garden of his dreams – one big enough for him to build greenhouses and cultivate his precious plants. He already owned a plot of land on the east side of Thornsett Road, on which he had built a shed for his plant pots and tools; and he now bought an extra plot in a neighbouring street, Wheathill Road. Without the commuting, he had more time to pursue this interest in gardening (which had begun in his days in King's Road, Chelsea), growing orchids and peaches, and he was a noted member of the Royal Horticultural Society. Indeed, the R.H.S. asked him to install the drainage system at its headquarters at Wisley.

The house was more than sufficient for him and Maria, and their two new live-in servants – their cook, Emma Hurst, and their young housemaid, Susan Killick. Life in their new home began well. By joining the local branch of the Freemasons he made useful business contacts in the area. The property was within half an hour's walk of the site that housed the Crystal Palace Exhibition, ever since its relocation there from Hyde Park in the winter of 1851. He spent his weekends at the Exhibition, studying the exciting gadgets and machines. And there was more: cycle racing, organ concerts, circuses, pantomimes, brass bands, firework displays with gigantic catherine wheels, penny slot machines, an aquarium, even a couple of giant dancing monkeys on swings.

Preparations were already under way for the Exhibition to celebrate Queen Victoria's diamond jubilee, sixty years on the throne.

But one afternoon in August, when they had been in their new home for almost a year, their maid, Susan, rushed into the house in a terrible state, full of news of a terrible accident she had witnessed at the Crystal Palace. A woman had been killed. The maid was on the Dolphin Terrace waiting to see a display of dancing and wire-walking, when three cars (or 'horseless carriages' as they were known) suddenly approached as if from nowhere. The third car was being driven in a crazy, zigzag, fashion. She heard the driver ring the car's bell and shout 'stand back!' The car swerved to miss a woman walking with her friends and a child; but instead of getting out of the way the woman moved into its path, putting up her umbrella and trying to shoo the car away just as if it were a horse! The next instant she was dead. The maid was still shaking even now, and Thomas and Maria gave her the rest of the day off. In the next few weeks Thomas read all about the incident in his local newspaper, the *Beckenham and Penge Advertiser*. It was one of the earliest reported fatalities involving a motor car, and it had happened practically on Thomas's doorstep.

Chapter 14

On the evening of Tuesday, 22nd January 1901, Queen Victoria died at Osborne House on the Isle of Wight. She was eighty-one years old and had reigned for sixty-three years, seven months and two days – longer than any British king or queen. The Queen had also outlived three of her nine children.

Church bells tolled across the country; news spread rapidly and even theatre performances came to an abrupt halt. Little knots of people gathered in silent groups in the streets, reading their evening newspapers, stunned by the gloomy headlines, many in tears. For most of them (unless they were very old) Queen Victoria had been the only monarch they had known. It was all a terrible shock and *very* unsettling.

Along Thornsett Road blinds stayed down, curtains remained drawn and lamps were turned down low. Almost every shop in Anerley displayed a black shutter, theatres were closed, and flags on public buildings flew at half-mast. In public people spoke in hushed whispers; birthday parties were postponed; locally, a meeting of teetotallers was disbanded, and the Ancient Order of Druids' annual dinner was cancelled. At the Marlboro' works Thomas put up black shutters and asked his workmen to give the railings a fresh coat of black paint. Maria made sure that their mourning clothes were washed and ironed, ready for them to wear at the Queen's funeral procession.

At six o'clock in the morning, on Saturday 2nd February, they took the West End of London & Crystal Palace Railway train from Norwood Junction station to London. Thomas was dressed all in black. Maria wore a fur cape and a black bonnet with black feathers. They felt snow flurries against their cheeks as they walked briskly through the streets. But even at this early hour there were already people up, dressed and outdoors. Both rich and poor felt they *had* to be at the Queen's funeral; it was as if a member of their own family had died. They could not simply stay at home.

The normal Saturday train service had been suspended and substituted by a Sunday timetable as a mark of respect. But that meant that the service was less frequent, and when the train pulled into the station it was already full, with up to sixteen passengers jammed into compartments only meant for eight. Thomas took Maria's arm and headed for the guard's van where they leaned against bicycles and cases and dozens of other passengers.

In London they found themselves on their feet again, queuing to board an omnibus which would take them to Paddington. When the vehicle arrived the passengers swarmed on, though this time Maria did manage to find a seat.

They drove past buildings draped with purple cashmere and white satin, colours especially chosen by Queen Victoria. The pavements were strewn with wreaths that had been sent from all over the country; it was said that there were enough for two wreaths to be placed on every lamp post along the route the procession would take.

It was still barely eight o'clock and only just light, but crowds already lined the streets. Boys had shinned up trees, and whole families had climbed on to the roofs of buildings and could be seen leaning against chimney stacks to obtain a better view. It was reckoned that a million people had come to London to pay their last respects.

Thomas and Maria squeezed themselves into a place close to the roadside in Park Lane, along the route the procession would take from Hyde Park to Marble Arch. But as the hours passed the crowd grew until it became twelve deep, and everyone was so close together that Thomas could not even reach into his pocket for his handkerchief. Men and women with expressions of sorrow on their faces drew up their collars against the biting wind as it lashed against their cheeks. Maria began to shiver. Thomas hoped she was not going to be ill. It was so cold here. Perhaps they should try to move to somewhere less exposed. He remembered a side road not far from Paddington station where they might have a better view. They managed to catch the last omnibus going west towards Paddington. It was a slow journey but it was worth the effort. They were able to find a much better view and it was not so exposed. Later they learned that the crowds had been sixty deep in Hyde Park. Thank goodness they had moved.

At last, sometime between half past eleven and twelve o'clock they heard the roll of drums in the distance. Then the light clip-clop of horses' hooves. There were little gasps of 'The Queen! The Queen!' Otherwise silence. Unlike many Londoners, they managed to see quite clearly the Queen's coffin as the gun carriage, pulled by eight cream coloured horses, rumbled past. They were glad they had made the effort

Thomas and Maria at Queen Victoria's funeral

to pay their last respects to the old Queen. Now the coffin would be put on the royal train and taken to Windsor where the Queen would be buried next to her beloved husband, Albert, who had died forty years earlier.

There was an eerie silence until around two

o'clock, when shops began to open throughout London. The couple were cold and thirsty and they might in normal circumstances have called at a tea shop for some refreshments; but they did not feel it was quite the right thing to do today. Instead they made their way back home. Maria felt exhausted but she assured Thomas she was very glad they had made the effort to go. There was a terrible sense of loss in the country as a whole. An age had come to an end. There was a new king. The late Queen's son, the Prince of Wales – in whose home Thomas had installed his finest cisterns, baths and plumbing – was now King Edward VII.

Chapter 15

Slowly things were returning to normal. Like many Londoners, Thomas and Maria enjoyed the display of Russian dancing, and the show put on by the dwarfs of the 'Lilliputian Theatre' at the Crystal Palace. But in the spring Maria's health began to deteriorate. At first it was just little things – she started to get tired quickly and became short of breath. Then her health became worse. Her feet began to swell, then her legs, making it hard for her to walk. Already a plump woman, her whole body became puffy and swollen. She started to suffer bouts of sickness and pain in the lower back. As these increased in frequency they were accompanied by fever and coughing. The doctor said that the problem lay with her kidneys which had become inflamed, and diagnosed Bright's disease, a serious condition of the kidneys, causing them to gradually fail. This may explain her swelling because the diseased kidneys no longer removed the body's excess fluid. Of course, nowadays doctors use water tablets, or diuretics, to spur the kidneys to remove the water but these had not been discovered then.

On Tuesday, 1ˢᵗ July 1902, Thomas wanted to show her all the latest summer 'specialities' at the Marlboro' works and showrooms. As walking was becoming more and more difficult for her, at first she declined. But when he seemed so disappointed she gave in, and they clambered aboard all the necessary omnibuses and trains to reach Chelsea.

Maria was impressed by what she saw. Apart from all the gleaming sanitary appliances, she was intrigued to see a telephone for the first time in her life. Thomas had just had one installed. In future, customers from hundreds of miles away could be put through to Thomas Crapper & Co. within minutes by asking the operator for 'No. 357 Kensington.'

Suddenly, when they reached the foundry, Maria had a coughing fit. It was so prolonged and she looked so ill that Thomas thought it best to cut the visit short and take her home, where the servants put her to bed and made her comfortable. At first she seemed to be better; but later that evening she complained of a severe headache and pins and needles running down the side of her face. Soon after this she completely lost the sense of feeling on the left hand side of her body.

Thomas thought that she must be having a stroke and called for the doctor. But before he could arrive Maria had lost consciousness. The doctor managed to detect a faint pulse, and for a while there seemed to be some hope. They tried to revive her with cold compresses and smelling salts. But it was all useless. The doctor turned to Thomas and said: 'There is no hope.' After half an hour her pulse ebbed away and he had to declare her dead. The doctor packed his bag and quietly left the room. Until this moment Thomas had held back but now the tears started to flow. He was overwhelmed. She had been a wonderful, caring wife to him. When he was ill she had nursed him. When he was worried she had listened to him. She had been more than he could ever have hoped for in a wife. They had never spent a night apart since their wedding day. He had loved her with all his heart. But she was now gone. What on earth would he do without her?

Four days later she was buried in Elmer's End Cemetery (now Beckenham Crematorium and Cemetery). The funeral was attended by various nephews and nieces who gave Thomas some comfort. The wreaths of white lilies that Thomas had chosen gave the only touch of brightness to an otherwise sombre day. Thomas and Maria were a wealthy but modest couple, so Maria's grave was a simple, long, low marble affair, although it was slightly larger than was usual: seven foot by three foot, instead of the standard six foot six inches by two foot six inches. In time, Thomas would be buried beside her.

After the funeral Thomas went back to an empty house in Thornsett Road. For several weeks after Maria's death, his great-nephew, Frank, stayed with him, until his nieces, Emma and May, were able to move to Thornsett Road to look after him. But he found life very lonely without Maria, and his business affairs pointless and exhausting.

In 1904, at the age of sixty-seven, he decided to retire. Without any children of his own, and with his brother long since dead, Thomas decided to pass the firm partly to his business partner, Robert Marr Wharam, and partly to his nephew, George, who he had always treated as the son he never had. By the end of the year there were eight shareholders in the business including various neighbours in Wandsworth and Kensington, but nearly all the shares were in the hands of George Crapper or the Wharam family.

Over the next three years the new owners built

what today we would call a 'flagship' store at No. 120, King's Road, Chelsea, close to Sloane Square. High street bathroom shops had not existed before this time. There were only plumbers' merchants for the trade, and they were generally to be found well away from busy shopping areas. When it came to sanitary ware, many people still tended to get easily embarrassed. Others, who could afford baths and sinks, for many years continued to prefer a strip-wash over a jug and bowl because they believed they would become ill by plunging themselves into a bath of water! Still others were worried that their ceilings and furniture might be ruined by leaks from water pipes installed throughout the house. It was all very distressing.

Matters were made even worse when they could see the cause of their concerns before their very eyes. The first time this had happened was more than thirty years earlier when Thomas Crapper had shocked the public by displaying toilet bowls in the windows of his shop in Marlborough Road. Now it was happening all over again and on a larger scale! A public display of gleaming white china toilet pans was easily visible at street level behind Thomas Crapper & Co.'s large plate glass windows in King's Road – not just some side street but one of the most

Ladies fainting at the sight of toilet bowls

important streets in London. For some ladies it was all too much and they became faint at such a shocking sight! Thomas would have chuckled at the prospect, but was not there to watch the spectacle. He was at home in Thornsett Road, Anerley, receiving visits from friends and relatives, a regular being his great niece, eighteen-year-old Edith Crapper who painted his portrait, a miniature which is now in the archives at the National Portrait Gallery.

In the months that followed, Thomas started to develop a series of ailments. When he ate he felt sick – which put him off his food. From time to time he experienced bouts of diarrhoea, followed by constipation. After going to the toilet he noticed blood and mucus in the pan. He wondered whether he might have an ulcer. For much of the winter of 1909 he had no energy at all, and stayed in bed suffering from acute pains in his stomach. By this time he had developed a tumour in his liver, which had caused his skin to become a peculiar yellow. Eventually he called the doctor who felt a lump in his stomach. After several visits he was told that he had bowel cancer and there was nothing that could be done.

On Thursday 27th January, 1910 Thomas died. His niece Emma, who was with him at the end, arranged the funeral. Four days later, following a ceremony in Holy Trinity Church, Anerley, he was buried by the side of Maria in Elmer's End Cemetery. His gravestone reads:

IN LOVING MEMORY

OF

THOMAS CRAPPER

WHO DIED JANUARY 27TH 1910

AGED 73 YEARS

Recently, a black and gold plaque with the following words has been added to the tomb:

> THOMAS CRAPPER
> INVENTOR AND
> SANITARY PIONEER
> FOUNDER (IN 1861) OF
> THOMAS CRAPPER & Co

At No. 12 Thornsett Road there is a blue plaque, put up by Bromley Council, although his date of birth is wrong. It reads:

> THOMAS
> CRAPPER
> 1837-1910
> engineer, developer of the
> controlled flow cistern
> lived here

At the time of his death Thomas Crapper was a

millionaire by today's money values. All his wealth he left to the children of his brother George. By doing this, he could thank him for his help in his early days in London, without which he would never have established his business.

The firm continued successfully through two world wars and three more reigns. It changed hands and moved premises, then, after 1969, it stopped trading for many years. In 1999 Thomas Crapper & Co. Ltd was acquired by a sanitary ware enthusiast and 'historian of the bathroom' and is trading again at Alscot Park, near Stratford-on-Avon, in Warwickshire, from where it continues to produce the finest bathroom fittings, 'ultra-authentic replicas' of the original designs by Thomas Crapper.

Today, two hundred miles further north of Thomas's resting place, in St Lawrence's Parish church at Hatfield near Thorne, there is a very unusual Millennium window. The window, which measures ten feet by twenty feet, and cost £40,000 to make, depicts a number of great moments in history, including the signing of Magna Carta; man landing on the moon; and, in memory of their most famous resident, a toilet pan, etched tastefully as a dark silhouette. It is a fitting tribute. For, although he certainly did not invent the flushing toilet, Thomas

Crapper was crucial in developing it and helped to increase its popularity. He achieved this through hard work, persuasive marketing and his friendly, good-natured manner which made his employees proud to work for him. During a period when bathroom fixtures were barely spoken of, he promoted the concept of plumbed-in sanitary ware, indoor lavatories and proper drainage. He invented the bathroom showroom where customers would come, look at the fittings in public and choose items for their home.

In his own way, Thomas Crapper did as much for sanitation as any law passed by the government. Those parts of the world today without clean water and flushing toilets have paid a terrible price in experiencing very high death rates. In late nineteenth century Britain, Thomas Crapper made a huge contribution to pioneering public health by affecting our everyday lives and promoting hygiene through practical measures. As *The Plumber and Journal of Heating* reported in the year he died, his company had succeeded in building up 'a unique reputation.' His showrooms and warehouses contained 'quite a galaxy of enterprise,' indeed everything possible 'to make the home comfortable and healthy.' He was a man who was ahead of his time.

Today, Thomas Crapper would have been in his

element. His name would be as familiar to us as Hitachi or Hoover. He would probably be running a chain of bathroom superstores, selling power showers, whirlpool baths, wet rooms and steam cabinets – leading the field once again. Perhaps he would be appearing on TV as a business expert in programmes such as *Dragons' Den*. So, remember, next time you use the loo and get that 'perfect flush', you are paying tribute to the foresight of Thomas Crapper, lavatory legend!

QUIZ

Now that you have finished the story, how much can you remember?

1. At the age of 15 Thomas was:
   (a) bunking off school in Thorne
   (b) in London with his brother
   (c) idling round the boatyards

2. His father worked as:
   (a) the captain of a paddle steamer
   (b) a plumber
   (c) a circus acrobat

3. To make ends meet, his mother took in:
   (a) prisoners on the run
   (b) dancing girls from the Doncaster music halls
   (c) ship stewardesses

4. When Thomas was an apprentice he had an attic room in:
    (a) Tottenham
    (b) West Ham
    (c) Chelsea

5. The areas with flushing toilets at the Great Exhibition were called:
    (a) cesspools
    (b) penny dreadfuls
    (c) halting stations

6. The year 1858 was known as the year of:
    (a) the Big Freeze
    (b) the Great Stink
    (c) Perpetual Darkness

7. In the mid 19th century, the River Thames was:
    (a) a source of clean, fresh water for the people of London
    (b) much loved by salmon fishers
    (c) a stinking public sewer

8. The engineer who built London's sewers was called:
    (a) Basil Fawlty

(b) Basil Brush

(c) Bazelgette

9. Thomas's self-raising toilet seat was nicknamed:
(a) the 'bottom slapper'
(b) the 'bottom pincher'
(c) the 'bottom crusher'

10. Thomas became ill with smallpox when:
(a) he was waiting for a train
(b) he was arguing with Robert Marr Wharam
(c) he was picking gigantic peaches in his greenhouse

11. Thomas's famous 'Water Waste Preventer' guaranteed:
(a) 'a lower water bill'
(b) 'satisfaction, or your money back'
(c) 'a certain flush with every pull'

12. At the Marlboro' works Thomas was known for his:
(a) ridiculous ties
(b) spotlessly clean shirts
(c) bad breath

13. Robert Marr Wharam was usually seen:
    (a) mending a cistern
    (b) with a can of beer in his hand
    (c) carrying an umbrella

14. When the Prince of Wales paid him a visit, Thomas was disappointed that he did not have:
    (a) a box of matches
    (b) toilet paper
    (c) a good joke ready to tell him

15. The Prince of Wales asked Thomas to make a special carved 'throne' water closet for his mistress whose name was:
    (a) Lily the Pink
    (b) Lily Savage
    (c) Lily Langtry

16. In the early 1890s Thomas was living in:
    (a) Bognor
    (b) Looe
    (c) Brighton

17. Maria and Thomas had to sack one of their cooks as:
    (a) dinner guests went down with food poisoning

(b) she was too fond of gin

(c) she became too fat to get through the kitchen door

18. Some ladies who saw the white toilet pans in Thomas's showrooms:
    (a) fainted
    (b) summoned the police
    (c) went in to ask if they could try them out

19. Thomas's grave can be seen today in a cemetery in:
    (a) Buckingham
    (b) Beckenham
    (c) Birmingham

20. At Hatfield in Yorkshire, Thomas is commemorated by:
    (a) the whole town flushing their toilets at 11a.m. on 27th January
    (b) a competition to see who can hurl toilet chains the furthest
    (c) a stained glass window showing a toilet pan

Wordsearch

a	t	h	o	r	n	s	e	t	t	r	o	a	d	n
i	s	h	m	s	e	w	e	r	s	y	n	c	o	d
r	i	p	o	a	w	a	l	t	o	n	o	i	c	a
o	t	l	d	m	h	o	x	r	r	a	t	a	h	o
t	i	u	o	m	a	g	k	e	o	i	g	e	i	r
c	h	m	c	e	r	s	n	m	b	r	n	s	l	r
i	c	b	k	w	h	a	c	i	l	a	i	l	b	e
v	n	e	e	i	o	s	h	r	r	m	v	e	l	t
n	o	r	r	l	e	x	s	n	a	d	o	h	a	s
e	r	e	s	m	e	d	o	n	m	p	n	c	i	a
e	b	w	a	t	e	r	s	i	d	e	p	a	n	m
u	h	h	a	d	n	e	s	r	e	m	l	e	s	k
q	t	e	e	r	t	s	t	r	e	b	o	r	r	c
e	r	t	u	b	e	r	c	u	l	o	s	i	s	u
g	b	i	l	l	y	c	o	c	k	r	u	d	d	b

Try to find: billycock, bronchitis, buckmaster road, chelsea, chilblains, dockers, don, elmers end, emma, great exhibition, maria, marlboro, ovington, plumber, queen victoria, robert street, rudd, sandringham, sewers, sloane, thames, thomas crapper, thornsett road, tuberculosis, walton, waterside, wc, yorkshire

Mystery Word

First you need to solve these questions. You only need one letter from each of your answers.

- Thomas's older brother and his nephew shared this name (1st letter) _____

- Surname of Thomas's business partner (2nd letter) _____

- It protects you from others copying your invention (5th letter) _____

- Disease Thomas had when he was living at Buckmaster Road (1st letter) _____

- First name of Thomas's wife (2nd letter) _____

- Old name for toilet paper (1st word, 3rd letter) - _____

- Square in Brighton where the Crappers lived (4th letter) _____

- Thomas was apprenticed to one (4th letter) _____

- Device that separates house drain from main drain (1st word, 1st letter) _____

- Thomas's name is on them at Westminster Abbey (1st word, 2nd letter) _____

- Tank that holds the water above the toilet pan (last letter) _____

The eleven letters are:

—— —— —— —— —— —— —— —— —— —— ——

Now rearrange the letters to make the mystery word:

—— —— —— —— —— —— —— —— —— —— ——

Key dates in the life of Thomas Crapper

1836   Crapper was born and baptized in Thorne, near Doncaster, Yorkshire.

1851   The Great Exhibition. Thomas was still at school in Thorne.

c.1853 He was apprenticed to his brother George, a plumber in Chelsea.

1858   'The Year of the Great Stink.'
        He began work as a journeyman plumber.

1860   He married his cousin Maria Green from Hemsby, Norfolk.

1861   He founded his own plumbing business at Marlboro' Cottages in Chelsea.
        He was now a 'master plumber.'
        A son, John Green Crapper, was born.

1862	Their baby son died.
1866	He built the first bathroom showroom in the world in Marlborough Road, Chelsea.
1867	They moved to No.1 Middleton Road, Clapham Junction, S.W. London.
1871	Thomas caught smallpox.
1872	He advertised boxes for 'curl papers' (toilet paper).
1874	They moved to No.8 Middleton Road.
1881	Patent for ventilating house drains.
1887	The Prince of Wales (the future King Edward VII) asked Thomas to supply the plumbing, including thirty lavatories, for Sandringham House.
1888	Patent for an improved disconnecting trap. Thomas and Maria were living at No.21 Powis Square, Brighton, with their niece, Emma, and two servants. Patent for Seat Action Automatic Flush.

1893   Patent for a foot lever operated water closet.

1895   He moved to No.12, Thornsett Road, Anerley, Kent.

1902   His wife, Maria, died.

1904   Thomas retired, passing the firm to his nephew George and his business partner Robert Marr Wharam.

1907   Thomas Crapper & Co. showroom opened at No. 120, King's Road, London.

1910   Thomas died and was buried in Elmer's End Cemetery, Beckenham.

Where to find out more about Thomas Crapper and his times

Books

Wallace Reyburn, *Flushed With Pride: The Story of Thomas Crapper* (Macdonald, 1969)

David J. Eveleigh, *Bogs, Baths & Basins* (Sutton, 2006)

Adam Hart-Davis, *Thunder, Flush and Thomas Crapper: an Encycloopedia.* (Michael O'Mara, 1997)

Helpful web pages

http://www.exnet.com/1995/11/01/science/science.html

http://www.jldr.com/crapper.htm

http://www.thomas-crapper.com/history02.asp

Places connected with Thomas Crapper

His previous homes:
Marlboro' Cottages, Chelsea
No.1 and No.8, Middleton Road (now Buckmaster Road), Battersea
No.21, Powis Square, Brighton, West Sussex
No.12, Thornsett Road, Anerley, London S.E.20

Thomas Crapper's grave in Elmer's End Cemetery (now Beckenham Crematorium & Cemetery).

Hatfield Church, Yorkshire, has a silhouette of a lavatory pan in a stained glass window in honour of the man, born locally. Also, the public loo in the church is a Crapper.

Sandringham House, Norfolk, and Westminster Abbey, London, have several Thomas Crapper manholes in the grounds.

'The Secret life of the Home' exhibition in the basement of the Science Museum, South Kensington, London, includes a working model of a Thomas Crapper & Co. 'water waste preventer' cistern.

Thomas Crapper & Co. Ltd, now based near Stratford-on-Avon, has a private collection of old W.C.s, basins, baths and taps, also salesmen's samples and period trade catalogues. This is not open to the public but they are happy to show their archives to interested visitors if an appointment is made in advance.

Glossary

cesspool   an open pit for household sewage.

chamber pot   a bowl with a handle, kept under the bed or in a bedside cabinet, and used as a urinal at night.

cistern   a tank to hold the water required to flush the toilet bowl.

closet chair   a chair that concealed a toilet.

disconnecting trap   a device that reduced the smell of sewage by breaking the connection between the house drains and the main sewer.

manhole   a hole giving access to a sewer and protected by a manhole cover.

night soil man a man whose job it was to empty privies and cesspits.

patent the exclusive rights granted to an inventor which prevent others from copying the invention.

privy a small building, usually in the back yard or at the bottom of the garden, containing a toilet seat mounted over a bucket or a large pit.

Thunderbox a completely panelled-in water closet, properly called a valve closet.

urinal a toilet, sometimes a trough, for males to urinate.

water waste preventer a toilet cistern operated by a syphon that prevented water leaks.

Toilet history

4000 BC   Toilets in Neolithic stone huts at Scara Brae in the Orkney Islands.

2000 BC   Toilets in private homes at Mohenjo-Daro, N-E India.
Egyptian latrine seat.

1450 BC   Palace toilets at Knossos, Crete.

0   Squat toilet with foot rests and drain hole, Sri Lanka.

315   There were 144 public toilets in Rome.

1358   Only four public toilets ('common privies') in London.

1449   In London Thomas Brightfield invented a type of toilet that flushed with water from a cistern.

1596	Sir John Harington built a flushing toilet in his house at Kelston, near Bath, Somerset.
1775	Alexander Cummings obtained a patent for improvements to the valve closet.
1778	Joseph Bramah perfected the design of the valve closet and produced thousands of them from his London factory.
1842	First toilet installed in Buckingham Palace.
1851	First public lavatory opened at The Great Exhibition in Hyde Park, London. Another opened in Fleet Street, London.
1852	First women's public lavatory, The Strand, London.
1857	The first toilet paper was sold (in squares) in Britain.
1870s	Valveless syphon prevented waste of water.
1871	Toilet paper was first sold in rolls in New York.

A selection of other words meaning toilet

backhouse
bathroom
biffy
bog
bucket and chuck it
can
chamber of commerce
cloakroom
close stool
closet
comfort station
crap house
crapper
dike
duffs
dunny (Australian)
facility
flash house

gents

halting station (Great Exhibition, 1851)

heads (Navy)

holy of holies

hopper

house of easement

jakes

Jericho

jerry

john

khazi

ladies

latrine

long drop

midden

necessarium

loo

netty

outhouse

powder room

(the) proverbial

privy

rest room

shit house

shot-tower

smallest room

the Geroge
the house where the king goes on foot
throne
throne room
Thunderbox
thunder mug
washroom
Waterloo

Go to the toilet

be excused
change my library book
check the plumbing
do a number one
do a number two
do something you can't do for me
drain the main vein
drop the kids at the pool
freshen up
go for a Jimmy Riddle
go for a leak
go for a piddle
go for a pony and trap
go for a tinkle
go for a Tom Tit
go for a widdle
pick a daisy
powder my nose
pluck a rose

point Percy at the porcelain
post a letter
see a friend off to the coast
see a man about a dog
see the geography of the house
shake hands with the unemployed
shake the dew off the lily
spend a penny
strain the potatoes
siphon the python
take a dump
telephone Hitler
to go somewhere
to go to the used beer department
to go where the wind is blowing
turn my bicycle around
wash my hands
water the tulips
wring my socks out

Answers

Quiz

1 (b)
2 (a)
3 (c)
4 (c)
5 (c)
6 (b)
7 (c)
8 (c)
9 (a)
10 (a)
11 (c)
12 (b)
13 (c)
14 (a)
15 (c)
16 (c)
17 (b)
18 (a)
19 (b)
20 (c)

Mystery Word

SANDRINGHAM

Acknowledgements

I would like to thank Simon Kirby of Thomas Crapper & Co. for letting me use archive sources and for generously sharing his expertise; Arthur Holden at Bromley Local Studies Library; Shona Milton at the Brighton History Centre; and Laurie Thorp from the Thorne Local History Society for their help in locating records. Dr Jessica Davison has been a mine of information on all matters medical. I would also like to thank Rebecca Epps, Emma Forge, Oliver St John-Jeffrey, Annamaria Pinazzi and Diana Williams for reading and commenting on earlier drafts of this book.

.